# Katie's Book

by Lynne Coulter
illustrated by Liz Alger

Harcourt
SCHOOL PUBLISHERS

Printed in Mexico

ISBN 10: 0-15-349987-7
ISBN 13: 978-0-15-349987-6

Ordering Options
ISBN 10: 0-15-349937-0 (Grade 2 ELL Collection)
ISBN 13: 978-0-15-349937-1 (Grade 2 ELL Collection)
ISBN 10: 0-15-357226-4 (package of 5)
ISBN 13: 978-0-15-357226-5 (package of 5)

1 2 3 4 5 6 7 8 9 10   050   15 14 13 12 11 10 09 08 07 06

Katie wanted to write a book. "I want to give it to Mom to celebrate her birthday," she thought. "What should the book be about?"

Katie's next-door neighbor looked over the fence. He was a writer.

"Hello, Mr. Phillips," said Katie. "What should I write my book about?"

"Here's some advice," said Mr. Phillips. "You should always write about things you know."

"I know about hamsters," thought Katie. She made a list of everything she knew about hamsters. The list wasn't very long.

"I know about cats," she thought. Her list about cats wasn't very long either.

Katie was still thinking about her book when Mr. Phillips looked over the fence again.

"What's the problem?" asked Mr. Phillips.

"I don't know enough about anything to write a book," said Katie.

"You know all about yourself," said Mr. Phillips. "You should write your own story."

"That's a great idea!" said
Katie. "I will write a book that is
about me!"

"Good luck," said Mr. Phillips.

Katie got to work. Her list about herself got longer and longer. Finally, she was ready to write.

It took Katie a week to write
her book.  She wrote all morning.
Sometimes she wrote all afternoon.

First, Katie showed the book to
Mr. Phillips. He loved it.

Then, Katie gave the book to her mom. Mom said the book was the best birthday present ever.

Katie was thrilled. She couldn't
stop smiling.

"If you ever want to write a
book, write about something you
know," Katie told Mom.

14

# Scaffolded Language Development

**STATEMENTS AND QUESTIONS** Review with children that statements are sentences that tell about something, and questions are sentences that ask something. Model the following examples from the book with correct intonation: *What should I write my book about? You should always write about things you know.* Point out that questions end in a question mark and statements end in a period. Then write the following statements on the board. Have children think of a question that each statement could answer. Write the questions on the board. Ask children to say each question chorally with the correct intonation and then answer the question with the statement.

1. I know about hamsters.
2. My book is about me.
3. I am eating an apple.
4. I am going to the park.

 ## Language Arts

**Write a Letter** Discuss with children how Mr. Phillips helped Katie in the book. Then guide children in writing a letter from Katie to Mr. Phillips to thank him for helping her.

 ### School-Home Connection

**Writing a Book** Have children tell family members about *Katie's Book.* Then suggest that children talk about what they would write about in a book.

**Word Count:** 254